Scrapbook of Memories
for my Daughter

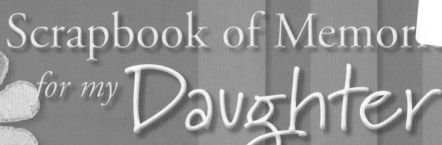

Surprisingly Simple
A LASTING GIFT of LOVE

PLACE YOUR PHOTO HERE

Made especially for

From

Date

INTEGRITY
PUBLISHERS

Scrapbook of Memories™ Series

Sisters *scrapbook of memories*

Grandmother's SCRAPBOOK OF MEMORIES

GRADUATE'S *Scrapbook of Memories*

Mom's SCRAPBOOK OF MEMORIES

Friends Scrapbook of Memories

Scrapbook of Memories *for my* **Daughter**

Scrapbook of Memories for my **SON**

Wedding SCRAPBOOK OF MEMORIES

Christmas Scrapbook of Memories

How to Create Your *Scrapbook of Memories*™

Acid-Free Paper

CONGRATULATIONS! You have found the perfect gift for your daughter! Just add memories, and you have a one-of-a-kind keepsake that will be treasured for a lifetime.

As you browse the pages of this scrapbook, think back over precious memories and unforgettable moments. As you fill each page with your thoughts, prayers, and remembrances, you are creating a customized token of love that can be enjoyed for years to come.

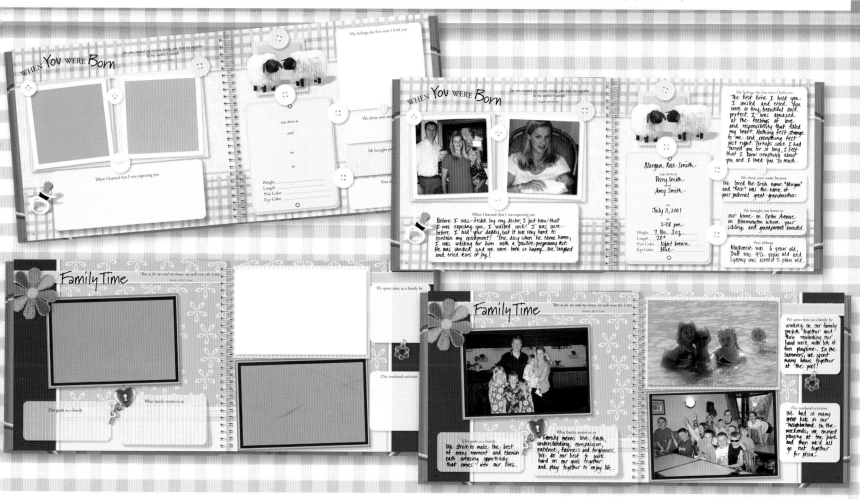

Look back over the special times you've had with your daughter, and record your memories with the help of the prompts provided on each page. (Unsure of some of the details? No problem! Save those prompts as a special opportunity to finish creating the scrapbook with the help of your daughter.)

Gather favorite photographs, and place them in the spaces provided.

3. Write a personal letter to your daughter in the space provided.

4. Tear out this page.

5. Save this Scrapbook of Memories for that special occasion, and then giggle, cry, and dream along with your daughter as you recall all of the precious memories you've shared together.

They'll never forget the gift of a Scrapbook of Memories!

A LETTER TO MY *Daughter*

_____

_____

_____

_____

_____

_____

_____

_____

_____

_____

_____

_____

_____

_____

_____

I thank my God upon every remembrance of you.

PHILIPPIANS 1:3 NCV

5

Your FAMILY Tree

Your Maternal Grandparents

_____

Date of Birth

_____

Place

_____

Aunts and Uncles

_____

_____

_____

_____

Cousins

_____

_____

_____

_____

_____

Mom

_____

Date of Birth

_____

Place

_____

Your Mother's Family

Dad

_____

Date of Birth

_____

Place

_____

Your Paternal Grandparents

_____

Date of Birth

_____

Place

_____

Aunts and Uncles

_____
_____
_____
_____

Your Father's Family

Cousins

_____
_____
_____
_____
_____
_____

7

WHEN You WERE Born

For you created my inmost being; you knit me together in my mother's womb.

PSALM 139:13 NIV

When I learned that I was expecting you

My feelings the first time I held you

_____
_____
_____
_____
_____
_____
_____
_____
_____
_____
_____
_____
_____

_____
was born to
_____
and
_____
on
_____
at (a.m./p.m.)
_____
at (location)
_____

Weight_____
Length _____
Hair Color _____
Eye Color _____

We chose your name because

_____
_____
_____
_____

We brought you home to

_____
_____
_____

Your siblings

_____
_____
_____

9

OH, Baby Girl!!

May your father and mother be glad;
may she who gave you birth rejoice!

PROVERBS 23:25 NIV

Your baby personality

Baby's eating and sleeping habits

Your favorite lullaby

A Gallery of Firsts:

Smile

Sit up

Crawl

Steps

Words

Playmates

Pet

Precious memories of your babyhood

Sugar AND Spice

Your toddler temperament

_____
_____
_____
_____

As a toddler, you enjoyed

_____
_____
_____

Toddler Favorites:

People

Game

Movie

TV show

Book

Song

Food

Toy

Bible story

Snuggle item

Bedtime prayer

Special memories of your toddler years

WHAT
Little Girls
ARE MADE OF

I have you in my heart.
PHILIPPIANS 1:7 NIV

I loved to watch you when

You said the funniest things

Your best wonder-filled questions

You loved to pretend

_____
_____
_____
_____

Childhood Firsts:

Learned to swim

_____
_____

Learned to ride a bicycle

_____
_____

Lost your first tooth

_____
_____

Sleepover

_____
_____

Learned to read

_____
_____

Mommy AND ME

When you and I were alone, we

_____
_____
_____
_____
_____
_____
_____
_____
_____
_____

Projects/crafts we've worked on

_____
_____
_____

YOU ME

*O*ur best times together

_____
_____
_____
_____
_____
_____
_____
_____
_____
_____
_____
_____
_____
_____
_____

Our mouths were filled with laughter,
our tongues with songs of joy.

PSALM 126:2 NIV

Mother-daughter time was special because

_____
_____
_____
_____

Daddy's LITTLE Girl

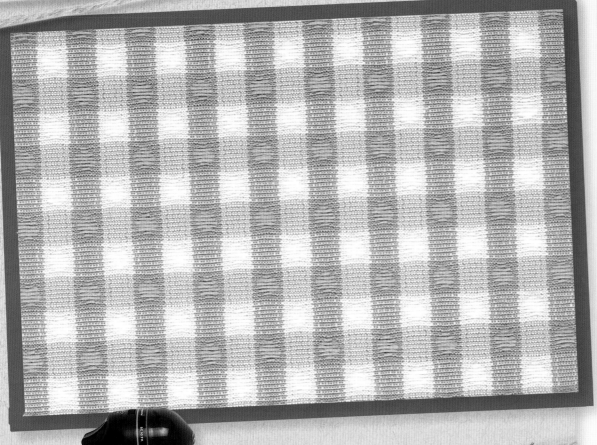

Dad's nickname(s) for you

The LORD has done great things for us, and we are filled with joy.

PSALM 126:3 NIV

Father-daughter time was special because

You and Dad had the most fun together

Special places Dad took you

Family Time

"But as for me and my house, we will serve the LORD."

JOSHUA 24:15 NASB

Our goals as a family

What family means to us

We spent time as a family by

_____
_____
_____
_____
_____
_____
_____

Our weekend activities

_____
_____
_____
_____
_____
_____

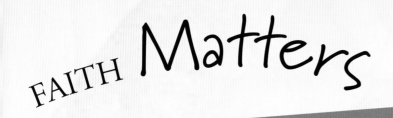

FAITH Matters

In our family, faith is

_____
_____
_____
_____
_____

The first time you knew God was real

_____
_____
_____
_____

The church we attended

_____
_____

Church groups you joined

_____
_____

*I'm eager to encourage you in your faith,
but I also want to be encouraged by yours.*

ROMANS 1:12 NLT

Favorite family scriptures

_____
_____
_____
_____
_____
_____

Blessed are the merciful

You were baptized/dedicated

FAMILY Vacations

Places our family vacationed

_____

_____

_____

_____

_____

_____

_____

Your favorite family vacation

_____

_____

_____

_____

_____

_____

In the summertime, you

Special visits with family and friends

CHILD's Play

What you liked to do for fun

_____
_____
_____
_____

You loved to play "dress-up"

_____
_____
_____
_____

Your favorite "adventures"

_____
_____
_____
_____
_____
_____
_____
_____
_____
_____
_____

When I was a child, I spake as
a child, I understood as a child,
I thought as a child: but when
I became a man, I put away
childish things.

1 CORINTHIANS 13:11 KJV

You caused mischief by

_____
_____
_____
_____
_____
_____
_____
_____
_____
_____
_____

When you grew up,
you wanted to be

_____
_____
_____
_____
_____
_____

A meaningful childhood
achievement

_____
_____
_____

TRYING Things OUT

A memorable event

Awards you received

Concerts/Performances

Sports you played (Sport/Year)

Lessons you took (Activity/Year)

Group activities (Activity/Year)

You ARE A STAR!

I loved to watch you

PLAYING *Favorites*

Be happy . . . while you are young, and let your heart give you joy in the days of your youth.

ECCLESIASTES 11:9 NIV

Movie

Color

TV Show

Book

Hobby

Bible Story

Type of Music

Pet

Possession

Place to Go

Way to Have Fun

Food FAVORITES

Restaurants we like

_____

_____

_____

Food Favorites:

Foods

Candy

Dessert

Snack food

Form of chocolate

Ice cream

Soda

Cravings

FASHION & Beauty

You should be known for the beauty that comes from within, the unfading beauty of a gentle and quiet spirit, which is so precious to God.

1 PETER 3:4 NLT

Your ideal shopping spree

Fashion trends

Best Looks

Where you like to shop

Are you spendy or thrifty?

Best place for bargains

A favorite "girls' day out"

Best Hairstyles

Beauty Secrets

Bad Hair Days

BEST Friends

A friend loves at all times.
PROVERBS 17:17 NKJV

Your best childhood friend(s)

You are a good friend because

Your group of friends now

I prayed for you and your friends when

God has blessed you with good friends

TEEN *Life*

What you did with your girlfriends

Your favorite pastime

You spent your weekends

Church youth group events

Fabulous Firsts:

Makeup

_____

Driver's license (Date)

_____

Car

_____

Date

_____

Kiss

_____

Job

_____

Whoever walks with the wise will become wise.

PROVERBS 13:20 NLT

DATING AND *Love*

*We love,
because He
first loved us.*

1 JOHN 4:19 NASB

When you started dating

Your first serious boyfriend

Memorable parties, dances or proms

God teaches us that love

BIRTHDAY
Revelry

On your first birthday

_____
_____
_____
_____
_____
_____
_____
_____
_____
_____
_____
_____
_____

"We had to celebrate this happy day."

LUKE 15:32 NLT

Age

Age

We liked to celebrate
birthdays by

Age

Age

UNFORGETTABLE Birthday PARTIES

Your favorite
birthday parties

What we did

_____
_____
_____
_____
_____
_____
_____

You invited

_____
_____
_____
_____
_____
_____

Holiday CELEBRATIONS

NEW YEAR'S EVE

We celebrated the New Year by

Our best New Year's Eve party

VALENTINE'S DAY

How we celebrated Valentine's Day

My favorite valentine you gave me

It was the sound of a great celebration!

PSALM 42:4 NLT

We celebrated Easter by

_____
_____
_____
_____

Easter services we attended

_____
_____
_____

Our traditional Easter meal

_____
_____
_____

Your favorite Easter dress

_____
_____

We decorated Easter eggs

_____
_____

MORE *Holiday* CELEBRATIONS

THE 4TH OF JULY

We celebrated the 4th of July by

_____

_____

_____

Our favorite fireworks display

_____

_____

_____

HALLOWEEN

On Halloween, we

_____

_____

_____

Your favorite Halloween costume

_____

_____

_____

Rejoice in the Lord always.

PHILIPPIANS 4:4 NIV

Thanksgiving

Thanks be to God for His indescribable gift!

2 CORINTHIANS 9:15 NIV

We celebrated Thanksgiving by

Our traditional Thanksgiving meal

Favorite Thanksgiving recipes

God has blessed our family

Favorite Thanksgiving recipes

MERRY Christmas

We celebrated
Christmas Eve with

_____
_____
_____
_____

When we opened
Christmas gifts

_____
_____
_____

On Christmas Day we

_____
_____
_____

Your best Christmas
present ever

_____

_____

_____

Favorite family Christmas photos

*Glory to God in the highest,
and on earth peace, good
will toward men.*

LUKE 2:14 KJV

Christmas TRADITIONS

Our family's Christmas traditions

"He will be called Immanuel (meaning, God is with us)."

MATTHEW 1:23 NLT

Christmas in our family means

Family Christmas favorites:

Programs/Concerts

Parties

Movies

Carols

Ornaments

We decorated the Christmas tree

What you loved most about Christmas

WARM *Christmas* MEMORIES

Our traditional Christmas meals

_____
_____
_____
_____
_____
_____
_____
_____

Family Christmas recipes

_____
_____
_____
_____
_____
_____
_____

We did our holiday baking

_____
_____
_____
_____
_____
_____

Family Christmas recipes

_____
_____
_____
_____
_____
_____

Ways our family helped others during
the holidays

_____
_____
_____
_____

*"For unto you is born this day in the
city of David a Saviour, which is
Christ the Lord."*

LUKE 2:11 KJV

Preschool & Kindergarten

Preschools you attended (dates)

Kindergarten you attended (dates)

Things you learned in kindergarten

O God, You have taught me from my youth.

PSALM 71:17 NKJV

On your very first day of school, you

Your favorite part of school

Elementary SCHOOL

The wise person makes learning a joy.
PROVERBS 15:2 NLT

School(s) attended

Favorite subject(s)

Favorite teacher(s)

Best school friends

What you loved about Elementary School

Middle SCHOOL

School(s) attended

Best subject(s)

Favorite teacher(s)

Best school friends

What you enjoyed about Middle School

_____
_____
_____
_____
_____
_____
_____
_____
_____
_____
_____
_____
_____
_____
_____
_____

Remember your Creator in the days of your youth.

ECCLESIASTES 12:1 NIV

Awards and recognition you earned

_____
_____
_____
_____
_____

I was especially proud of you when

_____
_____
_____
_____
_____
_____
_____
_____
_____
_____
_____
_____
_____
_____

High SCHOOL

"Be strong and do not give up, for your work will be rewarded."

2 Chronicles 15:7 NIV

School(s) you attended

_____

_____

Best subjects

_____

_____

High School friends

You excelled in

Math

English

Fun High School memories

USA GYMNA[...]

High School highlights

Youth Group trips

Your High School
Commencement
Ceremony was

_____

_____

_____

_____

High School graduation date

A+

I was so proud of you for

_____

_____

_____

_____

_____

_____

College

College(s) you attended

_____
_____
_____
_____

I devoted myself to study and to explore by wisdom all that is done under heaven.

ECCLESIASTES 1:13 NIV

During college, you lived

_____
_____

Jobs during college

_____

Your major(s)

Your minor(s)

Your best memories about college

OUR Relationship

Train up a child in the way he should go, And when he is old he will not depart from it.

PROVERBS 22:6 NKJV

We like to spend our time together

I love being your mom

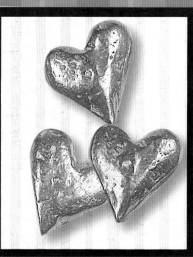

I hope I have taught you

_____
_____
_____
_____
_____
_____
_____
_____
_____
_____
_____
_____

It warms my heart to know

_____
_____
_____
_____

What you have taught me

_____
_____
_____
_____
_____
_____
_____
_____
_____
_____
_____

FAVORITE *Memories*

You made my day when

_____
_____
_____
_____

I laughed so hard when

_____
_____
_____
_____
_____
_____
_____

It was so fun when

_____
_____
_____

What I admire most in you

_____

_____

_____

_____

_____

_____

_____

_____

_____

_____

LIFE'S *Lessons*

I could have no greater joy than to hear that my children live in the truth.

3 JOHN 4 NLT

Things that came easy for you

_____
_____
_____
_____
_____
_____
_____
_____
_____

Special times when I have prayed for you

_____
_____
_____
_____

I was so proud of you when

Your most meaningful life lesson

I will always be here for you

MOM'S
Advice

The best advice I've been given

_____

_____

_____

_____

Love

_____

_____

_____

Growing Older

_____

_____

_____

Advice
to you on:

> *"When you go through deep waters and great trouble, I will be with you…. For I am the LORD, your God, the Holy One of Israel, your Savior."*
>
> ISAIAH 43:2–3 NLT

Enjoying Life

Faith

Parenting

What Matters Most

WITH *Love!*

If words could express my love for you

_____

_____

_____

_____

_____

_____

_____

_____

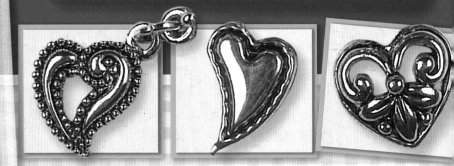

My dreams for your future

_____

_____

_____

_____

You will always be my little girl

_____

_____

_____

"The LORD make His face shine upon you,
And be gracious to you."

NUMBERS 6:25 NKJV

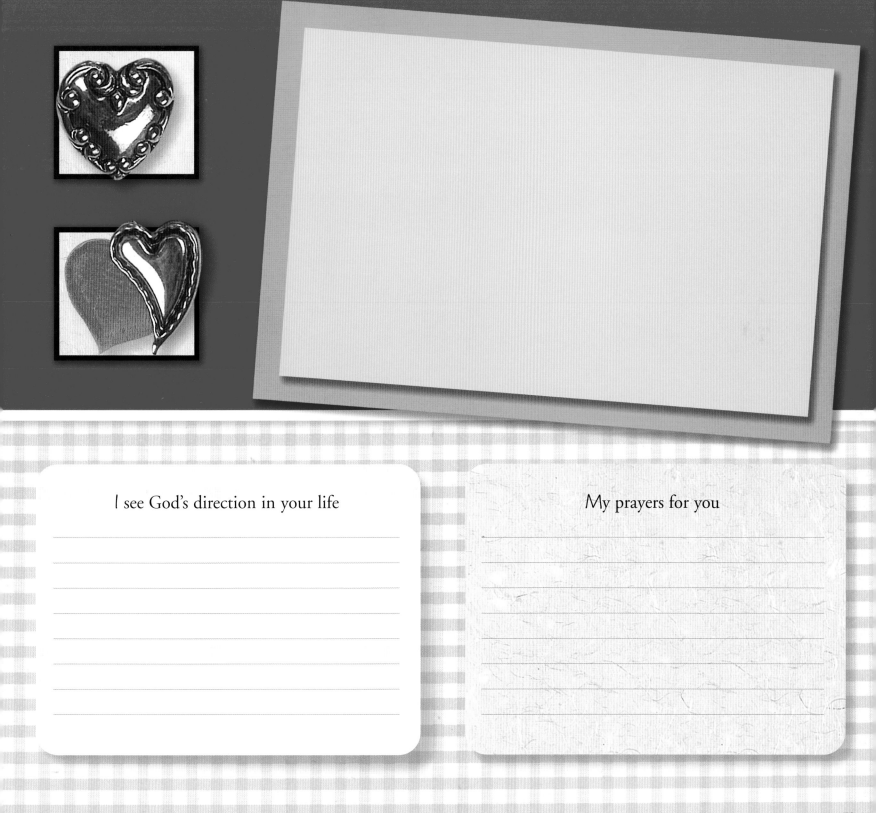

I see God's direction in your life

My prayers for you

SCRAPBOOK OF MEMORIES™
for my Daughter

Copyright © 2004 by Integrity Publishers
Published by Integrity Publishers
A division of Integrity Media, Inc.,
5250 Virginia Way, Suite 110,
Brentwood, TN 37027

HELPING PEOPLE WORLDWIDE EXPERIENCE
the MANIFEST PRESENCE of GOD

Scripture references are from the following sources:

The Holy Bible, New International Version (NIV). Copyright © 1973, 1978, 1984, International Bible Society. Used by permission of Zondervan Bible Publishers. The Holy Bible, New Century Version (NCV), © 1987, 1988, 1991 by Word Publishing, Nashville, Tennessee 37214. The New King James Version (NKJV), © 1979, 1980, 1982, Thomas Nelson Publishers, Inc. The *Holy Bible*, New Living Translation (NLT), © 1996 Tyndale House Publishers, Inc., Wheaton, Illinois 60189. New American Standard Bible (NASB), © 1960, 1977 by the Lockman Foundation. The Contemporary English Version (CEV) © 1991 by the American Bible Society. The King James Version of the Bible (KJV). Used by permission. All rights reserved.

Guide questions and editorial content by
AMY KOECHEL SMITH
Designed by Koechel Peterson & Associates, Inc.

Printed in China.
04 05 06 07 RRD 9 8 7 6 5 4 3 2 1